Hello! My Name Is Patrio

Vaughn had a difficult time concentrating on the assignment his teacher was discussing. His mind was full of thoughts of birds, many birds.

This was not the first day he had difficulty
thinking of the assignment for class.   These birds
Kept flying through his thoughts.

It was always the same Kind of bird. There was
good reason for this. The Magpie had won his
heart.

"The Magpie may have a brain the size of a pea, but the bird is very smart," he thought.

For a ten year old boy, the Magpie Chick presented him with magical dreams!

Imagine his surprise the day his best 'bird friend' held out her hands to him and said, "Here is a gift for you."

This was the most exciting day of all his days!

"Thank you," said Vaughn excitedly.

He asked permission, from his parents, to keep the bird. They agreed he could keep it if he would take very good care of it.

"What is the bird's name?" they asked.

"I can't call the bird 'Bird'," he thought.

He thought and thought and thought.

"His name is Patrio," he answered.

From that day, and forever, the bird was known as 'Patrio'.

To be a proud owner of a Magpie Chick required one to be very responsible.

Any bird owner knew that a bird, just like a child, needed to be fed, kept clean, have a comfortable home and most of all.....loved.

So Vaughn prepared a box and placed it in a clean dry place in his room. This would be the bird's new home.

Baby Chicks have Mothers to feed them, but this chick had no Mother.

The baby would have to be fed often during the day and during the night.

An alarm clock was used to wake Vaughn.
His parents were pleased with the way he woke himself every few hours and fed the baby with an eyedropper.

"If magpies can recognize themselves in mirrors and can imitate other bird calls, then my bird will learn how to imitate what I say," said the boy.

Very often Vaughn would talk to Patrio. "Hello, my name is Patrio," he would tell the bird.

Time and time again you would hear the boy talking to the beloved bird, "Hello, my name is Patrio."

"Hello, my name is Patrio," said the bird one day.

"Mother, Father, everybody please come here!" screamed Vaughn.

"Patrio just talked! Patrio just talked!"

Father, Mother, brothers and sister joined in the excitement.

Patrio must have realized how much everyone loved him, for from that time on, he said those same words all of the time.

Each day he grew in words and body size.

The mother would call her daughter to help with the dinner. "Vicky, Vicky Jean! Please come help Mother with the dinner," she would call out.

It was a pleasant surprise when Patrio began to scream the words, "Vicky! Vicky Jean!"

Patrio loved to sit on the bedroom window sill and look outside.

Then a sad day came into the life of the young boy.

"Mother," he said, "I cannot keep Patrio locked in my room anymore.

He looks out the window. He pecks at the window. I think he wants to get out with other birds."

"Vaughn," Mother replied lovingly, "I have learned a saying from a Chinese Proverb.

"What is that Mother?" asked Vaughn. Mother replied, "I have heard it said this way, when you love something very much and you let it go, it will return to you if it truly loves you."

Vaughn thought about this proverb for some time and then asked, "Mother, what if Patrio doesn't come back?"

"Then this will be a test of love," replied the Mother.

Vaughn thought about this test. This was a very difficult test.

Patrio was set free into the world he saw through the closed window.

The ten year old was praying that patrio would love him and return.

What do you think Vaughn saw as he looked out his window the next day?

Whom do you think was calling, "Hello! My name is Patrio!" Patrio returned each day.

Vaughn knew that he was truly loved by his Magpie.

Patrio and the boy grew in lasting friendship and love.

The Magpie seemed to enjoy his freedom. One could see him flying from house to house.

The neighbors were surprised that he could talk. To some it was a little frightening to hear a bird talking. But once they knew it was Vaughn's bird Patrio, they felt comfortable to reply with "Well, good morning Patrio. How are you today?"

When Mother would hang clothes on the line to dry, Patrio would try to help by pecking at the clothes pins.

Patrio would help Mother while she was picking raspberries by trying to untie her shoelaces.

He was very smart and was able to untie her shoelaces many times.

Vaughn could not wait to come home from school to play with Patrio. The Magpie acted just as excited to see the boy when he came home from school each day.

The bird would come to the back fence to visit Vaughn. He was always happy when Vaughn would give him food.

Patrio's favorite place to sit was on Vaughn's arm. Then the conversation began.

Vaughn and the Magpie talked and laughed.

Their moments were magical and memorable. This was not a time Vaughn would forget, nor would he want to forget. This was a special part of his journey through life.

Patrio would come to the front window to visit with Mother and peck at the window while she washed dishes.

He enjoyed talking with her. "Hello! My name is Patrio," he would say.

This conversation would happen time and time again.

He met other Magpies and would bring them home
to the fence. You could hear them chatter. He was
a very happy bird.

One day Patrio flew home. This was a different kind
of visit.

He sat on the window sill and he was very quiet.
Neither Mother nor the bird talked.

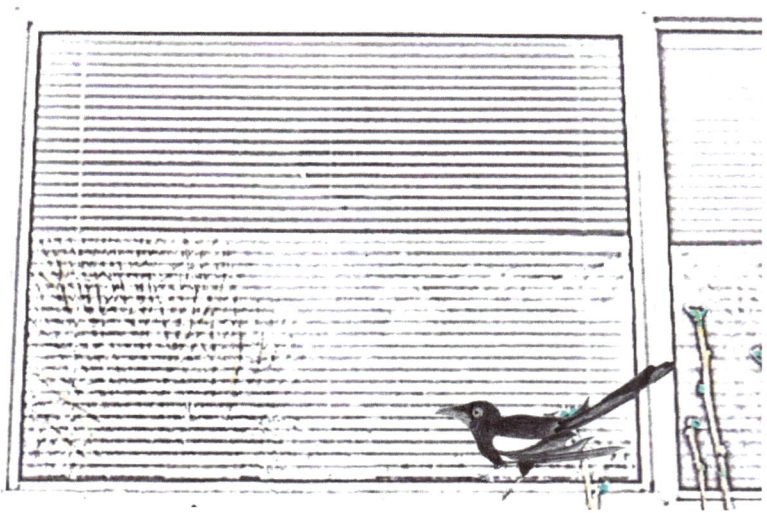

Patrio pecked at the window. He pecked at the
window again. Mother looked up and stopped
washing the dishes.

"What is the matter Patrio?" asked Mother. "Don't
you feel like chatting with me today?"

Something was wrong. Mother could tell that he was ill because Patrio was not speaking to her.

Mother went to the window, picked up Patrio and cupped him in her hands. The Magpie was carried into the Living Room to the place where Vaughn was lying. Vaughn was ill so Mother carried the bird to him. He and Patrio spent time together. All afternoon the boy and his bird were lying side by side.

When Patrio died the little boy cried.

The Mother cried also.

Vaughn and Mother made a resting place for the bird, in a shoe box.

A piece of white satin was cut to fit into the bottom of the box. It was shiny, soft and white. They lined the sides of the box with white satin and then gently placed the tiny body inside, on the soft lining.

A satin-lined lid was place on top of the box.

Patrio was at peace.

All of the family members said good-bye to Patrio.

The Father buried the bird in a beautiful spot in the family's back yard.

How happy they were to have been friends with
this talking Magpie.

Memories of his love remained.

Mother and Vaughn were happy to see Magpies on the fence each year.

Vaughn remembered the friend's gift she had held in her hands, that special day a long time ago.

He thought of the times he had set his alarm clock and filled the eye dropper.

He remembered the Chinese Proverb his Mother told him and the test of love. He felt warm inside to think that he and Patrio passed that test of love.

Mother and Vaughn listened carefully as the Magpies chattered.

Maybe if they listened closely, just maybe, they would hear one of these Magpies calling,

"Hello! My name is Patrio."